Preface

The word "nani" means splendid, pretty, or better word is there to describe the nēnē, or Hawaiian goose, one of the rarest geese on earth. It is native to the Hawaiian Islands and can only be found there and a few other places, where it has been artificially introduced. Its closest living relative is the Canada goose. Approximately one half million years ago a common ancestor of the Canada goose and the nēnē arrived on the Islands of Hawai'i. Finding a moderate climate, they never left. Over the course of thousands of years the birds began to change. No longer migratory, their wings became shorter. The rocky terrain they encountered led to the development of strong legs and toes, and has resulted in a reduction of the webbing between their toes. They became predominantly terrestrial, and although they still swim, they do so less frequently than many geese. The birds were plentiful until man began to develop the islands. Importation of the mongoose, pigs, and domestic cats led to decimation of nests. Overzealous hunting added to the stress on these beautiful birds. By 1952, there were fewer than 50 birds left. Extensive conservation efforts have contributed to a significant increase in the nēnē population. In 1957, the nēnē became the official bird of the Territory of Hawai'i, eventually becoming the State Bird when Hawai'i was admitted to the Union in1959.[1] Continued, long-term conservation efforts will be required if the nēnē is to survive, and thrive in the future.

In this story of rhyme, an adult nēnē reminisces
about its mother's tales of nēnē history. She refers
endearingly to her goslings as "nani nā nēnē,"
or beautiful Hawaiian geese.

I owe a debt of gratitude to
the staff at the national parks of Hawai'i
for their guidance and assistance
in completing this book.

This book
is dedicated
to people of the world,
working together
to create new beginnings
and
second chances...

DrDADBooks is a registered trademark of Children's Wildlife Books by
Daniel A D'Auria MD

ISBN10/ISBN13 9781548332914/1548332917

Nani nā Nēnē

Written and Photographed
by
Daniel A D'Auria, MD

All photographs taken on the Island of Hawai'i
and at the
WWT Slimbridge Wetlands Centre

DrDADBooks.com

A simple story I will tell
Of geese that do on islands dwell
"nēnē" or "Hawaiian Geese"
For eons here they've lived in peace.

2

I still hear Mother long ago
To goslings much too young to know
"Nani nā nēnē," she would say
"Be safe when you are out at play."

She'd tell us stories of the past
About how nēnē came, at last
To these islands, wild and free
Of volcanoes from the sea.

Half a million years ago
A wayward winter wind did blow
Ancient geese out to the sea
And to a land called Hawai'i.

They found a climate, warm and mild
Without long winters, harsh and wild
A place where they could settle down
No need to migrate round and round.

Over time their wings did change
Without the need to fly long range
They didn't need wings of such strength
To fly long distances, at length.

A rough and rocky land they'd found
So stronger legs to get around
And walk on ancient lava flows
So stronger grew their nails and toes.

The webbing used for swimming round
Between their toes could still be found

But rough terrain on which they trounced
Had left that webbing less pronounced.

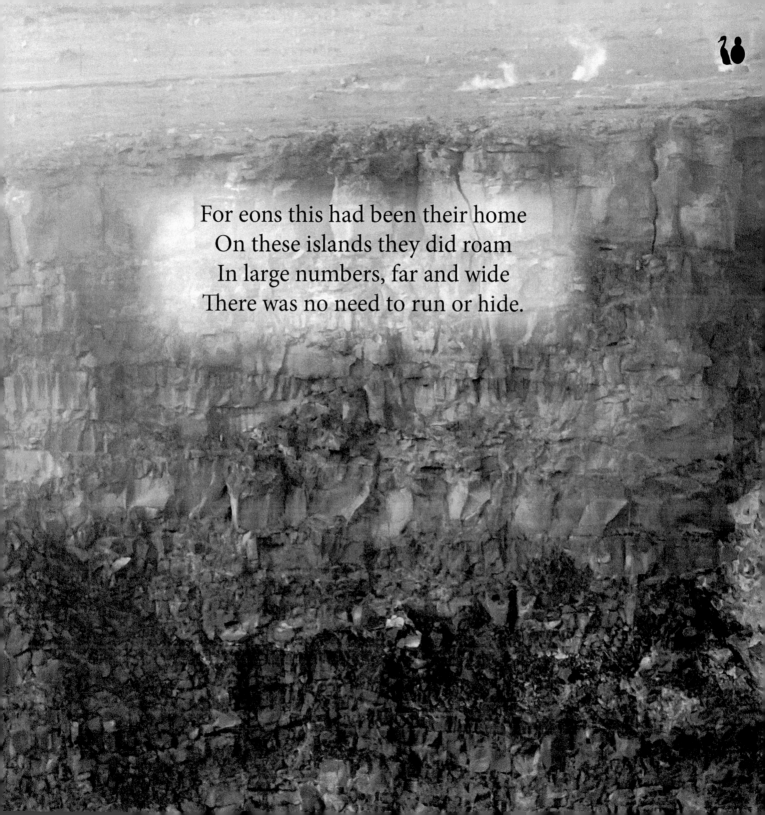

For eons this had been their home
On these islands they did roam
In large numbers, far and wide
There was no need to run or hide.

Then one day, from distant shores
Strange predators arrived in scores
New people and the things they'd brought
Meant changes to what had been taught.

The land in which they lived was changed
Their nests and nestlings rearranged.
"Nani nā Nēnē," mothers taught
But all their lessons seemed for naught.

21

22

23

By late in nineteen fifty two
The nēnē numbered just a few.
All the changes had a cost
It seemed that nēnē would be lost.

Suddenly, when we'd lost hope
Some humans dared to help us cope.
They tried to help us overcome
From things that had us overrun.

The efforts that they've made are grand
To give us back the upper hand
But some things cannot be undone
This struggle won't be simply won.

We'll need the help of more of you
To help restore a balance to
This land of islands we call home
To make it safe for all to roam.

"Nani nā nēnē!" mothers call
There is no need to run at all.
For humans lend a helping hand
To nēnē living in this land!

National Parks

Before western civilization forever changed Hawai'i, tens of thousands of nēnē existed on the islands. By the late 1940s, only a few dozen Hawaiian geese survived. Research began in an effort to understand the reasons for the decrease in the goose population and to try to determine if anything could be done to help assure their survival. With the assistance of researchers and conservationists from around the world, the territory of Hawai'i began a captive breeding and reintroduction program that has resulted in establishment of a significant nēnē population.

The factors that hinder their survival
still exist today.
Credit should be given to the staff of the
Hawaiʻi national parks and
dedicated groups of voluteers who
support programs
that help to maintain the nēnē population.
I owe a great debt of gratitude
to the staff
of the national parks of Hawaiʻi
for introducing me to the nēnē of Hawaiʻi
and to this great story of conservation.

In 1946, Peter Scott (son of the Antarctic Explorer Captain Scott) opened Slimbridge, the first of what would become nine wetland centers across the UK, dedicated to the advancement of science and conservation of wetland habitats.

The Slimbridge Center became intimately involved in conservation efforts to save the dwindling nēnē population of Hawaiʻi.

The nēnē population had fallen to just 30 geese, and scientists were not certain if the remaining genetic pool would sustain the species.

Much research over decades has
helped reestablish the nēnē
and other endangered species
around the world.
Many of the nēnē reared at Slimbridge
were flown back to Hawai'i
and released into the wild.
Joint captive breeding programmes
and active field conservation
work typifies
WWT's approach to conservation of
threatened waterfowl.

This book would not have been possible
without the gracious help and support of the
WWT Slimbridge Wetland Centre
in England and its dedicated staff.
I thank them for allowing me access to their
grounds and their nani nā nēnē.

Page Number Key

Nēnē

Some of the rarest geese in the world deserve special numbers for their pages, so I created goose-like number designs. Numbers zero and eight are eggs, while all the others are silhoutte sketches of geese.

1 = 1   4 = 4   7 = 7   10 =10
2 = 2   5 = 5   8 = 8   11 =11
3 = 3   6 = 6   9 = 9   12 =12

[1]United States, Department of the Interior, *1957 Annual Report: The Governor of Hawaii to the Secretary of the Interior For the Fiscal Year Ending June 30, 1957* (Washington: GPO, 1957), p. 54, accessed February 21, 2015, http://hdl.handle.net/2027/uma.ark:/13960/t9b575b66. As well as a reference to the nēnē becoming the official bird of the territory of Hawai'i, this report includes information pertaining to the territory's wildlife management and research in 1957. With regard to Hawaii's admission as a state, United States Senate bill S. 50 outlined provisions for the transition.

Section 15 decreed that existing laws of a territory at the time of admission to the union would remain in force, thus maintaining the nēnē's official status in the transition. This information is found in United States, Cong. Senate, *Committee on Interior and Insular Affairs Statehood for Hawaii: Hearings Before the Committee on Interior and Insular Affairs*, 85th Cong., 1st sess. (Washington: GPO, 1957), p. 95, accessed February 21, 2015, http://hdl.handle.net/2027/mdp.39015082044366.

I would like to thank my wife, Kimberly Martin, a consummate professor of history, for this reference, her research, and her endless support.

54109230R00027

Made in the USA
San Bernardino, CA
07 October 2017